Like Yourself Again!

To Don and Debbie;
Love you all and thank you so much for your prayers.
Becky 7/19/03

Like Yourself Again!

A Simple Approach for Overcoming Alcohol Abuse

Becky Nelson

Foreword by
Dr. Richard Honaker

Brown Books Dallas, Texas

Like Yourself Again!

Printed and bound in the United States of America.

For information please contact Brown Books
16200 North Dallas Parkway, Suite 225, Dallas, Texas 75248
972-381-0009 www.brownbooks.com

First Printing 2002

ISBN 0-9719235-0-7

LCCN 2002091686

Dedicated to

Bevan and Stoney
(of course)

Contents

Foreword

Having known Becky Nelson and having seen her through some of the tough times, I could summarize this foreword as "the biography of a success story."

In fact, this book is a story of success, and Ms. Nelson tells it in a practical, warm, reasonable manner, with courageous and insightful references to her own struggle. In the pages of this book she will take you along her path to sobriety. She will tell you how she got to where she was and how she finally came to be where she is now. Along the way she offers an impressive array of self-help mechanisms, highlighted by practicality, thoughtfulness and personal experience.

For those readers struggling with alcoholism, substance abuse, or maintaining their own form of recovery, this book is essential. The "feel good" that comes from it will sustain you through your tough times. The practical applications will help you at 3:00 A.M. when nothing else is there to help you.

I have seen Ms. Nelson at her worst and at her best. She, like many people, was a functional alcoholic. Her path through this valley led to major changes in her life and her lifestyle. Had she had this book as a guide to live by, her struggle and search would have gone much more easily and much more quickly. To that end, she has chosen to help others "get well" more quickly and permanently by putting her path to recovery in writing.

There are many ways to approach your problem, but I dare say that this is one of the best I have seen. As you read this book you will find it hopeful, inspiring, and, most of all, practical. It will hit you right in the face with the reality of what you are up against, and hopefully you will come out of it with the same success as the author.

I commend you for your effort and desire. I hope for your healthy success.

Richard A. Honaker, M.D., F.A.A.F.P.

Acknowledgments

Thanks so much to my friends and family for their ongoing support for this project. Thanks especially to John Ater and Milli Brown and her staff at Brown Books. This book would never have been written without their talents, expertise, and compassion.

Introduction

This book is for the millions of people in America who know that they are drinking too much alcohol and don't know what to do about it.

Our society offers little in the way of treatment for alcohol abuse aside from AA and long-term substance abuse programs. Neither of these choices were an option for me. Although I am an outgoing and successful businesswoman, standing before a group of strangers admitting that I was suffering from an incurable disease and that I was helpless to fight it was terrifying. That's not how I felt and I couldn't see the benefit of public humiliation in order to get help. The long-term substance abuse centers were equally frightening. Missing weeks (or months) from work would mean involving my employer and would also be embarrassing. The benefits of these programs just didn't seem to be there; for their success rate to me is not good. AA admits that 95 percent of the people who attend their meetings eventually drop out and the number of people who quit the substance abuse clinics is 50 to 70 percent. [1]

On ABC's "20/20" program, Dr. Nancy Snyderman stated, "It is clear now that current treatment methods benefit only a small number of those who desperately need help. It is time to begin a dialogue about other options–new roads to recovery." This book is intended to begin that dialogue. It offers an alternative that is positive and personal. Alcohol abuse is personal, and it is important to understand yourself and then determine the changes that you need to make to take it out of your life. You know that you are drinking too much. You don't necessarily like drinking anymore, but your body is accustomed to the drug, and your lifestyle makes the use of alcohol rather easy, so it's just more convenient to keep drinking. Right? Absolutely! I was there. In my case, I saw my face aging and was overweight for the first time in my life. I was angry, irritable, tired—the list goes on. Even with that, the decision to continue drinking won over the alternative. To the rest of the world I was an outgoing, successful, and confident person. Inside, I knew that I couldn't attend even the simplest meeting without at least one glass of wine. Hopefully, you are reading this book before you have reached that stage of drinking. If you are there already, I hope you will be able to relate to my experiences and avoid repeating my mistakes.

If you are only at the "drinking four or five beers every day" stage, applying the principles in my book should be much easier for you, if you *want* to stop. Knowing that you want to stop drinking is a big

1 Alternatives to Abstinence, http://abcnews.go.com/onair/2020/2020_000607_alcohol_feature.html

thing and is especially important for that "little more than social drinking" stage. You believe that you don't *have* to have those beers every night; it's just how you are. You can quit any time. You are a very productive, successful person. Life couldn't be better; you have everything that you could ask for, right?

Then why are you drinking? Is it just a habit? Are you only a social drinker? What is a social drinker? Do you drink every day? The average American man drinks two drinks a day and the average woman drinks one per day. Do you exceed the average? If so, that's more than social drinking, and it may already be a habit. It is an unhealthy and very dangerous one. Break it now. It positively will get worse before it gets better.

When I see people who drink every day but insist that they are only social drinkers, I get a feeling of remorse. I'm not making judgments against them; I only wish that they could see things through my eyes. I look at the degradation of my life from the time that I was at that stage of drinking until I finally stopped, and I would not wish that experience on anybody! I want to scream at them and say, "Stop now, when it's so much easier! Don't wait until your body is damaged. Don't wait until you have to drink to relieve the withdrawal symptoms. Stop now, when it will be so much easier."

Maybe I should repeat: "Stop now, when it will be so much easier!"

I want to shout it from rooftops! Please learn from my experiences. Alcohol addiction is a progressive disease that if untreated will slowly and gradually destroy your life. Take control now *before* the problems begin.

Problems will begin to surface in your life if they haven't already. Things like your spouse being upset because you stayed out too late may not be a big deal now, but wait until it begins to happen more and more often.

You may begin to experience agitation and increased stress, and soon some health problems will surface. Hopefully, you have not yet experienced problems at work associated with drinking, or run-ins with the law (DWI, public intoxication, auto accidents). Even the most careful drinkers will begin having problems in their lives that are associated with alcohol.

> *There are all sorts of self-tests that you can take to help determine if you are a problem drinker. You can take them all, answering questions like, "Do you drink to over-come hangover symptoms?" "Do you undergo a personality change when you drink?" The question that really matters is, "Do you drink every day?"*

Don't wait until you are at the drinking all day, everyday stage (like me). It's horrible, and when I look back at the wasted days of my life because I kept on drinking instead of *living*, it makes me sick. I don't even want to think about the damage that I did to my family, especially my children. That is too painful even now.

One thing is critical for you to grasp in order to stop drinking, and it is something that no one can give you, say to you, or do for you. You have to have the DESIRE. You really have to be fed up with the alcohol-dominated lifestyle that you are living and be ready to move on. If you are not there yet, at least read the book; so when your time comes you will have a place to start.

The process absolutely begins and ends with you. A thousand conscious, sub-conscious, and/or genetic reasons may cause your drinking, but it is your mind that creates the desire and functionality to pick up that drink every day. Why? Ask yourself that question and you can begin the process.

Let's face it, when you look for ways to stop drinking, the list of alternatives is rather limited. Most options are embarrassing, time-consuming, costly, and downright frightening. *Very* frightening.

That's why I wrote this book. I look at the positive side of sobriety. Rather than count my past days of sobriety, I want to concentrate on the many full days that I have ahead of me. I say full, because it's amazing how much more I can get out of a day when I'm sober. I had completely forgotten that life does continue past 9:00 P.M. When I was drinking, I could never stay awake past 9:00 P.M. Now I find that my most enjoyable hours are from 9:00 P.M. to 11:00 P.M. when the kids are in bed, and it is finally my time to read, watch TV, do my nails, work out, prepare for tomorrow, or whatever I want to do.

A sober lifestyle is so much more fulfilling, and hopefully *Like Yourself Again* will show you that it is *not hard* to stop drinking. With the help of a physician, some guidelines, and some new habits, you can soon see the advantages of sobriety and really like yourself again. (We'll work on the love part in another book.)

Good luck. No matter what stage of drinking you are in, things will get worse before they get better. You may not believe that and neither did I. I was the worst, with the attitude of, "I can be a social drinker. I just need to cut down." It may be that something truly tragic has to happen in your life before you realize that you need to stop. That is the basis of the "hit rock bottom" theory, which I also dispute. Stop now, and begin enjoying the benefits of sobriety now. Life is so much better. I promise.

Introduction

My Story

I began drinking the same ways millions of people do: socially. And I was very social! Beginning in college and carrying through until my first real job out of college, I partied. Very well. In college it was all the sorority/fraternity functions, and after college it was all the happy hours after work. Two years after school, I joined the sales division of a large communications corporation, which provided me with my dream job. My successes were triumphantly received, since women were not typically successful in my field. My career moved quickly, as did my appetite for alcohol.

I was single, with lots of time to drink with the guys after work, which I did about three times a week. The other nights I would buy a six-pack of beer and a bottle of wine and go sit in my apartment. I purchased an electronic piano with a headset (to allow me privacy when I played) and felt that it was perfectly normal for me to sit down with my beer and wine and play the piano for several hours of enjoyment every night—every night that I wasn't at happy hour, that is. Soon I was drinking every day for some reason or another. This scenario is scary enough, but then I met my future husband.

This man was born and raised a Dallasite and came from a lovely, old Dallas family. His mother soon became my best friend, and when our first child was born, our bond only became stronger. We spent hours dressing him up, shopping for him, planning upcoming events to show him off and a great many hours just staring at him in wonder. He was (and still is) so beautiful, and my life was filled with so much love, I could not imagine anyone being happier.

My career continued to flourish. I was promoted to regional sales manager when I was twenty-nine years old and Stoney (my son) was six months old. My new position was much more demanding, and my husband and I made the decision that he would care for our son with the help of a full-time housekeeper in order to make up for the time that I had to be gone. That was our first mistake. The arrangement worked well at first. As a matter of fact, we had a second child, our daughter Bevan, two years later.

Ours was an unconventional lifestyle, but it worked for us. My husband was able to do fun stuff with the kids; I had full-time house help and an exciting career. Everything was going great.

Did we drink? Yes, we drank every day. There were many social opportunities to drink. We would take the kids out to dinner and have drinks or go to happy hour or spend a quiet evening with wine at home. But we drank every day.

Things started degenerating when my father-in-law passed away in 1987. Grief, family conflict like I've never seen before, and lots of anxiety related to the settling of the estate were the order of the day. We also began to worry about my mother-in-law's health and the effect of all this on her. At that point, drinking became much more than an acceptable social thing.

My husband inherited a large sum of money from his father's estate. The money proved to be a major pivotal point in our lives. We joined an exclusive country club, began to take great trips, and planned only the best for our children. Sounds great, right? Wrong.

Golf at the country club became an everyday occurrence for my husband. His drinking was quickly approaching the dangerous stage, as was mine. He played and drank all day while I was at work.

In the evening, I prepared dinner and spent time with the kids while drinking several beers and at least one bottle of wine per night. My husband would come in, eat, and go to bed. I was okay with that, because I was tired and only wanted to spend time with the kids. We lived like that for a while, until the drinking began to present problems in our lives—big problems.

I was arrested for driving while intoxicated in 1989 as I was returning from a dinner/dance at the country club. Because of an influential lawyer from the club, I was given a slap on the wrist and a $1,000 fine. My husband, however, had repeated incidents with the law, and those caused a great deal of stress for our family. I stood by his side and supported him every time, and there were many. I covered for him constantly for everything from hit-and-run accidents and DWIs to embarrassing situations at the school and other social functions.

Social Services once visited us after my husband was reported for drinking when he picked our son up at an after-school program.

During that period, we went through so many humiliating and degrading incidents, and each time we vowed to cut back or stop drinking altogether.

In 1994, I began begging and pleading with my husband to stop drinking. That year, we lost his mother, which was very painful for both of us. At that point, we decided to buy a new, larger house so we could concentrate on something fun, rather than grieve for something that we couldn't change. Though we didn't know it, we had reached the beginning of the end.

The month that we moved into our new home, the bank that handled my husband's trust fund sent a letter stating that no disbursements would be made until certain estate matters were settled. Suddenly, money became an issue, though not a crippling one. We could survive on my salary until the bank resolved the questions, although it would not be pleasant. In addition, my husband's license was revoked for one year due to his DWIs. That was really a problem.

His truck needed repairs, but we decided that repairs were senseless since he couldn't legally drive. He became totally dependent on me for transportation. This caused me a great deal of trouble at work because I would take him to the bus stop around noon, and he would go directly to the club. He would either take a taxi home, or call me to pick him up somewhere.

Our lives rapidly became very dysfunctional. I enabled him to continue with his horrible lifestyle, and every day I was drinking more myself. Our arguments and fights became angrier and uglier. My resentment toward him was so maxed out that I couldn't stand him. It was bad enough that I had to get him where he wanted to go, concentrate on my own job, and take care of the kids, but then he would return home drunk, angry, and defensive. This clearly was when the horrible stuff started.

The Horrible Stuff

The year I just described was 1995. I kept thinking that if we could get through the year, everything would be okay. My husband's anger was becoming excessive because sober or drunk he was always angry at something. My life was unbearable. I begged and pleaded with him to stop drinking, but to no avail. He became defensive and his comment was that I was not one to talk. He was absolutely right, by the way. It was hard for me to insist that he stop if I was not willing to do the same. It was a vicious circle, but I had married for better, for worse, in sickness and in health. We were both sick, and I was sticking with him.

To his credit, by the way, he is a wonderful man without the booze. He has a heart as big as all outdoors and would give his last dollar to anyone who needed it (I've seen him do it a thousand times). I loved him, and the thought of divorcing him when he needed me most was unthinkable. I knew that if we could get through 1995, things would be okay.

As predicted, in December the bank freed up some funds at the same time that my husband's license was reinstated. YES! We went out and bought a brand new minivan so that we would have a vehicle for traveling, transporting kids, and so forth, now that it was legal for him to drive again. By January 1996, we were set. We thought everything would be fine.

In February 1996, my best friend was coming to town! There was a big party planned at a Dallas country club to celebrate another friend's fortieth birthday. Everyone was excited; new clothes, hairstyles, and the works for the grand occasion. We did some prepartying the night before (my husband was unable to attend, of course, because it was past 6:00 P.M., which means that he was already too drunk), and I really enjoyed seeing our old friends. The next day, my friend and I spent the day preparing for the party.

I had not talked to my husband much that day and began to worry that he would not be home in time to dress for the evening. I decided to lie down for a nap around 4:00 P.M., and we were to leave around 7:00.

At 4:30 another dear friend who lives in my same small town used her key to come into my house to wake me up. She was there to give me the distressing news that my husband had been arrested for another DWI. Because of past offenses, we could not bail him out until the next morning. My friend's husband had already made those inquiries.

I dressed, attended the party alone, and explained that my husband's golf game had gone on a little longer that anticipated, and that he was unable to attend. I'm sure everyone assumed that he was simply too drunk, so the lie was readily received.

I stayed at the party, continuing to cover up my totally dysfunctional life. Inside, I felt completely and totally empty. Have you ever felt like there are no bones or blood or organs inside your body? That you are totally empty? I drank my wine wondering how it could be flowing in my body without veins and intestines. I was hollow and that was how I felt that entire evening. The amount of alcohol that I had that night and for many nights to follow became inconsequential. I could no longer feel.

The next day my husband returned, completely dejected and depressed. I spent the afternoon with my friend, still hiding the facts about my situation. I worked very hard to portray a normal life to my friends and family, a normal reaction for me. Cover up, denial, nonacceptance, and enabler—all those words applied. My feelings of overwhelming loss took over everything else. I was tired, sick and tired, and had no clue how to repair my crumbling life.

The Really Horrible Stuff

I couldn't bring myself to help my husband with his current situation. I was too disgusted and fed up. I had no place to turn. I began drinking wine first thing in the morning, returning home for lunch so that I could drink more wine. Then it was back to work until happy hour, when I would get my next fix, definitely a requirement for my body by then.

By the time I got home, I could barely stay awake to feed the kids and get them in bed by 9:00 P.M., and then I would pass out too. Shortly, I developed a new bad habit. I started waking up about 1:00 A.M., watching old TV shows all night, drinking wine all the while. Hopefully, by 4:00 A.M., I would go to sleep before getting up at 6:30 when it was time to start all over again.

This horrible cycle continued for several months. In the meantime, I continued to look for ways to make my husband see how unhappy I was. Even at this point, divorce was not a consideration. I felt that I was in an incorrigible situation and I had to just live with it. I was terribly unhappy and depressed, and felt totally helpless.

About this time I finally did a smart thing. I decided that I had problems and that I was not dealing with them properly, so I made an appointment with a counselor/psychiatrist/shrink. Dr. Eubanks, later referred to as my highly paid best friend, did help me. It took some time, but he made me see that I had to separate myself from my husband and his problems. How could I do that? He was my husband, the father of my children, and his problems were mine.

Dr. Eubanks made me see that we are all responsible for helping ourselves, especially when it comes to substance abuse. My husband had to take responsibility for his mistakes, and I needed to take responsibility for mine as well. My responsibility was to my children, and I could not continue to see to their upbringing and welfare with the deteriorating environment in our home. During the initial months of my psychotherapy, we concentrated on ways to save my marriage. I continued to try to make my husband see how his drinking was affecting our lives, but since I was abusing alcohol at approximately the same rate, he discounted my opinions. Finally, in October Dr. Eubanks suggested that there were a few occasions when divorce was acceptable and advisable, and our situation was one of them. I was not ready to take that step. I loved my husband and knew that if we could just overcome the drinking, we could stay together.

I began praying every night and every morning that God would deliver a solution to me. I knew that I needed to stop drinking, but with the circumstances, I didn't know how. Alcoholics Anonymous intimidated me. If I checked myself into a rehab program, people at work would know (as if they didn't all suspect anyway). I didn't know what to do. I prayed to God to help me find a way, and I believe that He delivered.

I began having stomach problems. I mentioned it to my physician who gave me some medication and suggested that it was probably due to my drinking. He knew that I drank too much, but he had no idea just how much. Once he asked me how much I drank a day, and I told him four to five glasses of wine (a very conservative estimate on my part). He looked surprised and asked, "How do you stay so pretty and drink that much wine?" I was pleased that I had been so successful in hiding my alcohol abuse.

The whole year became a big blur for me. My son began to get into trouble. At age eleven, he got into fights at school and participated in the standard "toilet papering" of various homes in the neighborhood, which later turned to egging houses, putting glue on doorknobs, trampling flowers, and the "ring and run" prank, all very annoying to our neighbors.

We began to receive anonymous telephone calls and letters from neighbors expressing their annoyance about my son's behavior and also the condition of our lawn. My feelings of humiliation, loss, and confusion were overwhelming.

I really wanted to be a good neighbor, but I became so lost in my drinking and the associated problems that I didn't know what to do. Of course, our lawn was a mess and so was the inside of our home. The regular occurrences of angry outbursts wreak havoc on a home. We were constantly repairing broken mirrors, furniture, windows, and holes in the walls.

One of my worst memories of that year was when a repairman came to repair the eight-foot window next to our back door. Shattered glass was everywhere, and it was obvious that it was done deliberately from the inside. It cost $165 to replace the window, and I remember writing the check in total despair. My eleven-year-old son had broken the window. How could a child have so much anger that he could do something like that?

I asked the question, but of course I already knew the answer. That was the behavior that he was being taught. He saw his father act like that every night, and I allowed and accepted it, and that sent the message to my son that such behavior was acceptable. How else would he act? Christmas that year was horrible. We had no family to spend it with, which was just as well since no one would have wanted to be around us anyway. I was drinking all day, every day and just didn't want to live anymore. My husband sat down with our personal phone list and called people all over the country that we hadn't seen in years. It was so obvious that he was drunk that I found those calls very humiliating. He called my parents and I wouldn't even get on the phone. My mother knew that something was terribly wrong, but felt as helpless as I did. The kids have since referred to that as their happiest Christmas.

I never could figure out how that could have been happy for them, but eventually they explained that they got more presents than ever that year. Of course they did. All we had to give them during that time were material things. We were so miserable and empty inside that we weren't capable of giving them the purity of our love, since there was no purity in our love. We loved them unconditionally and deeply but were not capable of providing them with what they needed most, security and stability.

In the meantime, my stomach pains continued. The medication that my physician prescribed helped for a while, but I felt really horrible all the time. My life was still a big mess, my drinking was totally out of control, and I was beginning to have problems at work. It was stressful to drink every day. I constantly wondered if I smelled like alcohol, constantly brushed my teeth at work, and worried if I was acting okay. Worrying about my next drink only added to my stress.

I carried wine with me on business trips, on airplanes, and always had extra bottles at home and in my car. I rotated liquor stores because I was so embarrassed that the store workers would realize how much wine I was actually drinking.

Also, I was so fat! I had never been overweight in my life until then. All the alcohol and no exercise were really taking a toll on my body. I was a nervous wreck and finally decided it was time to stop drinking.

In January 1997, I simply could not go on any further. My will to live decreased daily. I continued to pray to God to show me the way to get out of my miserable life. I knew I had to find a way to change or give up and die. The answer finally came.

I went back to see Dr. Honaker, my physician. I explained to him that I realized my problems were caused by drinking and asked him to help me stop. I explained I was fed up with my alcohol-plagued life, but that I needed his help with the physical addiction part. I still lied about the amount of alcohol that I was drinking, but he of course agreed to help me.

He gave me a sedative to ease the withdrawal symptoms and told me to go off the wine gradually, over a two-week period. I began the program as he suggested, drinking only two glasses of wine a day. I was uncomfortable and pretty shaky, but at least I felt good about what I was finally doing.

After about three or four days, the pain in my stomach intensified dramatically. I called Dr. Honaker and he sent me different medicines. I tried various medications, but the longer I went without alcohol, the stronger the pain became. After six days, the pain became unbearable and my doctor insisted on seeing me again. After seeing me in his office, he immediately admitted me into our local hospital. Diagnosis: acute pancreatitis.

The first two days in the hospital I was allowed nothing to eat or drink. Not even ice. I underwent several tests to better diagnose my problem, but after the third day I started getting better. Thankfully, I had not done any permanent damage to my pancreas or my liver. On the third day I was finally given water and some chicken broth for dinner, and eventually I was served three meals a day, all liquid, with some Jell-O for dessert. I realized that I was detoxing. What my body needed was a good rest and a good cleansing.

Dr. Honaker spoke with me several times regarding my alcoholism. He insisted that I go to AA or find some way to break my drinking habit. I promised him that I would, but I really didn't know specifically how. He was concerned that I didn't have a plan and was afraid that if I had just one drink, the cravings would be so strong that I would begin drinking every day again. He said that I couldn't be a social drinker. As an alcoholic, a chemical imbalance existed in my brain that made me crave alcohol, and if I had even one drink, the horrible addiction cycle would begin again.

I believed everything he said and became intrigued with the clinical definitions of alcoholism and its effects on brain chemistry. As usual, I questioned. There is no history of alcoholism in my family. My parents never drank and I rarely even saw alcohol until I was an adult. I didn't understand all of the information, but knew that I needed to learn more.

Fortunately, there was no permanent damage to any of my organs, and I was so grateful to finally be cleansed of all the alcohol in my system. I knew that I had been given another chance, and I was not going to jeopardize my health again.

As my condition improved, the specialists quit coming, and all the tests stopped. My doctor kept me there for five days, until I could take the pain medication for my stomach orally as opposed to intravenously. Dr. Honaker came to see me the day that I was released and told me quite firmly, "Now go fix the problems in your life and don't ever take another drink." I promised him that I wouldn't and then thanked him for saving my life.

My Story

Chapter 1

WHY DO I DRINK and Is It Time To Stop?

Answering the question "Why do I drink?" is the hardest part of the process. It requires a great deal of soul-searching. Get to know yourself. One of my favorite life philosophies from my "psuedo hippy" days is that I have to love myself before I can expect someone else to love me.

How many of us really love ourselves? It's not an easy thing to do, but it is something that we must strive to achieve. Sure, we go through periods of life that are not fun, and maybe we used to love ourselves, but do we still?

It's so easy to fall into a rut, especially when you are in your thirties or forties, which are the most common ages to abuse alcohol. In many cases, the kids are out of the cute stage where they do all those adorable things, the job has become a little mundane, and you have accepted that this is all there really is to the "career thing." You could be facing the loss of a loved one, struggling in your marriage, experiencing financial problems, a job loss—the list could go on and on. You have problems, and just as your problems are unique to you, the way that you deal with them is also unique.

Look into your past life, your present life, and your future. What would you like to change? Why are you drinking? In most cases, the drinking is a way to hide from the realities of your mundane or, in my case, horrible life. You have created a vicious circle between your unhappy life and the results of overdrinking. You drink because you want to escape; yet the problems remain. You have heard it before, and it's exactly what's happening. You have poor health, agitation, low self-esteem, and a bad attitude toward life.

If you are drinking to overcome hangover symptoms, the circle has come full around. You are either drunk or hungover most of the time. It took a long time for my doctor to convince me that alcohol was adding to my stress instead of easing it, but he finally convinced me.

If you look at the way alcohol is broken down in your system, the added stress makes sense. A small percentage of the alcohol that you drink goes directly to your breath and urine. The rest is digested throughout your body and does really bad things. Your kidneys work overtime and still end up sharing the burden of the poison with your liver, which really takes a beating, especially with women. Women's bodies tend to be smaller and more susceptible to the effects of alcohol abuse. Your nervous system gets really out of whack because it's reacting to the major metabolism change and goes from really shaky to "can't move anymore."

Think about your body. Look at pictures of the human anatomy and understand what is going on inside you when you drink. See if you can feel it.

You can feel the shakes. I still fear those today, they were so terrible. How about that empty-headed feeling, when you feel "fuzzy" and it's hard to concentrate? Alcohol affects everyone in different ways, but most of the ways are not pleasant. Other than the initial "high" that you feel when you are drunk, the negatives far outweigh the positives. In my case, I don't know that I even still felt the high. My drinking was more for medicinal purposes, and when I did have a good time drunk, I usually couldn't remember it very well the next day. Not a good thing!

Okay, let's look at the statistics. Do you drink because you were an abused child? (Sixty percent of women alcoholics were abused as children.) Do you come from a family of drinkers? Are you prone to problem drinking because of genetic makeup? This brings up the controversy of genetics versus environment. There are some valid theories that certain microorganisms increase the number of enzymes that create an alcohol-craving metabolism, which is how alcoholism is genetically carried through generations. Some research indicates that alcoholism is strictly an environmentally learned behavior. Either way, understanding your cravings and where they come from will help you gain control of the addiction.

None of this really matters, unless it helps you identify why you drink. You are one individual. Just as your reasons for drinking are unique, the way alcohol affects your body and mind is also unique. You are the only one who can identify your problems and can feel their physical and emotional effects. Take control. It's not easy. As I said, this is the hardest thing that you have to do. Make up your mind that you are going to fix what is wrong in your life and that you are going to do it sober. Trust me, it is so much easier than tackling those issues while you are drinking. Doesn't that sound crazy?

If someone had told me that I had to stop drinking and then kick my husband out, file for divorce, defend my rights for full custody of my children, face financial problems, all without drinking, I would have said "No way! I need that crutch now more than ever!" Wrong. Take control of your life, lose the crutch, and then face the problems with a clear head (and body).

Scared? Of course you are. It's only natural to be frightened about making such an important life change. This may help.

Make a list of the reasons that you do *not* want to stop drinking. Identify your fears. The easy thing to do is to continue drinking, but is that what you really want? Try to analyze *specifically* what frightens you. Make your list. It won't be hard.

My list included things like:

Will I be able to sleep at night?

How do I explain not drinking at social and work events?

What effect will this have on my social life?

How will I control those awful shakes?

How do I get the courage to make that group presentation?

How will I get through each day?

It is scary, but it is more frightening to think of drinking for the rest of your life. That's right, if you don't stop now, when will you? Does something truly tragic have to happen in your life to make you stop? The time is now. The longer you wait, the more difficult it will be. That is a fact!

While you are at it, think about the benefits of not drinking. List these as well. Which list is shorter? Can you think of even one? It is hard to think of the benefits of sobriety when you are so lost in the addiction, but try. It's okay if you cannot think of many, just make your list and put it away. In thirty days, try the exercise again and compare the results.

My list included things like:

> I will feel better physically.
>
> I won't wake up with a hangover.
>
> I will remember what I did last night.
>
> I will go to sleep rather than passing out.

So, when is the time to stop? What has to happen to make you stop? Consider these facts:

In the United States, alcohol accounts for 975,000 deaths each year from alcohol-related traffic accidents, alcohol-related murders, suicides, and non-motor-vehicle accidents. This is 50 percent of all auto deaths, 60 percent of all drownings, 70 to 80 percent of all deaths in fires, and 85 percent of liver deaths.

Suicide and alcohol are linked. From 7 to 21 percent of all alcoholics commit suicide. Just over two-thirds of all suicide attempts are alcohol-related. Suicide is the second-leading cause of death in teens under eighteen and people over sixty-five. [2]

2 Judy Monroe, *Alcohol*, Springfield, NJ, Enslow Publishers, Inc., 1994, p. 29

Now you say, "Right, but none of those things would happen to me. I don't drive drunk, and I'm certainly not going to commit suicide." Accidental deaths can happen any time and any place, but no one can argue with the statistics that show those things are more likely to happen when alcohol is present.

Think again about your body. Do you realize the damage that you cause to your body when you drink more than one drink in one hour? A typical liver can only process about one-half ounce of alcohol per hour. Clearly, over time excessive drinking can affect not only the liver, but also many organs in your body. Here are some of the ways:

> LIVER DAMAGE – Heavy drinking can severely damage the liver, causing fatty liver, alcoholic hepatitis, and cirrhosis. About 15 to 35 percent of moderate to heavy drinkers develop extra fat in their livers. Then their livers cannot process alcohol or other foods as fast. Fatty liver disease kills more than 1,000 people each year. However, if people stop drinking, their fatty livers will heal over time. [3]

> CIRRHOSIS – a permanent, dangerous disease kills liver cells. This disease slows the blood flow through the liver. Eventually, the liver could fail. Over 14,000 people die each year from cirrhosis. It is the ninth leading cause of death in the United States. [4]

3 Ibid, p. 30
4 Ibid, p. 30

Heart Damage – Alcohol can affect the heart muscle so that the heart may degenerate, scar and enlarge, or beat irregularly. It can also raise blood pressure and heart rate. This places a great demand on the heart and increases the risk of stroke or heart attack.

Pancreatitis – The pancreas is a small organ near the upper part of the stomach. Pancreatitis, inflammation of the pancreas, is a serious illness. It causes vomiting, stomach pain, and nausea. About 40 percent of people with pancreatitis are alcoholics. [5]

Cancer – Since alcohol affects the immune system; it increases the risk of cancers, especially of the mouth, throat, liver, and bladder. Studies show an increased risk for breast cancer in women alcoholics. Alcohol is a factor in over 7,000 cases of cancer each year. [6]

Brain Damage – Heavy alcohol consumption is a well-documented cause of brain damage, according to a 1990 report by the National Institute of Alcohol Abuse and Alcoholism.[7] Alcohol abuse is linked to memory loss, depression, anxiety, seizures, blackouts, and hallucinations. During blackouts, drinkers do not actually lose consciousness but cannot remember what happened during a drinking episode. Chronic alcohol abuse damages brain and nervous system cells, perhaps permanently.

5 Ibid, p. 30
6 Ibid, p. 30
7 Ibid, p. 29

AIDS – Research shows that alcohol injures the immune system, the system that protects the body from disease. Heavy drinkers suffer more infections and cancers than nonalcoholics do. This may mean that heavy drinkers could increase their chances of getting HIV if exposed to it; and if a drinker already has HIV, alcohol could increase the risk of his or her developing AIDS.

Malnutrition – Alcoholics or chronic heavy drinkers may starve because they often prefer drinking to eating. Alcohol interferes with the body's use of vitamins and minerals. It blocks the body's ability to absorb vitamins C and A, resulting in anemia and reduced resistance to disease. Doctors often find chronic alcohol abusers low in potassium, magnesium, calcium, folic acid, and thiamin.

Deficiencies in these areas can cause the following:

Potassium – Muscle weakness and irregular heartbeats.

Magnesium – Weakened bones, poor muscle contraction, poor use of food by the body.

Calcium – Double the loss of normal calcium excretion, which could lead to weakened bones.

Folic Acid – Anemia, hair loss, skin changes, decreased healing of the skin, decreased sense of taste.

Thiamin – Muscle degeneration, heart irregularities, weight loss, and fatigue.

Osteoporosis – Heavy drinking impairs calcium absorption. This increases the risk of osteoporosis, also known as brittle bones disease. The body needs calcium to build and repair bone. Osteoporosis affects twenty-five million Americans, usually those over fifty years old.

Stomach and Ulcer Problems – Because alcohol irritates the stomach lining, heavy alcohol use can cause heartburn, upset stomach and inflammation. It increases the risk of ulcers and makes existing ulcers worse.

After you have answered the questions of why you drink and when to stop, consider the risks that you take when you stop. Risks? Making the decision to stop drinking is risky? It may sound crazy, but you are risking loss of a familiar lifestyle, certain friendships, dependence on alcohol, and other things. Be prepared for these changes in your new life and be confident that you are making the correct choices.

Risks are not bad; they are good. Risk-taking is very underrated. It is mentally stimulating (whether you win or lose) and it makes simple tasks, as well as giant projects, more exciting.

Consider this poem from the Healthy Habits Web page:

Risks

To laugh is to risk appearing the fool.
To weep is to risk appearing sentimental.
To reach out for another is to risk involvement.
To expose feeling is to risk exposing your true self.
To place your ideas, your dream, before a crowd is to risk their loss.
To love is to risk not being loved in return.
To live is to risk dying.
To hope is to risk despair.
To try is to risk failure.
But risks must be taken,
because the greatest hazard in life is to risk nothing.
The person who risks nothing,
does nothing, has nothing, and is nothing.
They may avoid suffering and sorrow,
but they cannot learn, feel, change, grow, love, live.
Chained by their attitudes, they are a slave;
they have forfeited their freedom.
Only a person who risks is truly free.

Author unknown

Can you answer these questions?

> If you could do anything and not fail, what would it be?
>
> If you found out that you had only six months to live, what would you do?
>
> Where would you go?
>
> Who would you see?
>
> What are you doing now that will lead you to fulfilling these dreams?

Take some risks. It's healthy, but don't go crazy. Remember to include logic in your decisions. Are you less scared?

Another important thing to remember when you begin to make changes is that you can change only things that *you can affect*. Don't make your goals dependent on anybody else. You are the CEO of your mind and body, but you have little effect on others' behavior (excluding kids of course!)

This may not be an easy thing to remember, especially if you are married or living with a significant other. Everybody's *time* to stop drinking is different. You must decide when the time is right for you, and you must respect others' decisions as well (even if they are your closest friend, lover, or spouse).

Make your decision to stop drinking based on your personal goals and within your time frame. Don't rely on others to motivate you, and don't expect your goals to motivate others. These are your issues, and you must be the one to confront them.

Set realistic goals for success, and determine an appropriate time frame. Do you need to keep your family members' goals in mind while setting your own? Absolutely.

Do you need to depend on friends' and family members' behavior to attain your goals? No.

These are *your* principles, *your* commitment to *your* rules. You don't have to discuss them with anybody. As a matter of fact, it may be best to keep them secret at first. People may try to discourage you (not meaning to, of course) but you may find that by *not drinking* you will intimidate some friends. This may sound crazy, but drinkers like to be around other drinkers. They don't want to be reminded about stupid things that they did by someone who was not doing them. Think about it. Be prepared for that, and discuss your intentions only with your closest friends and/or family members.

Chapter 2

Go to a Doctor and Be Prepared!

Before you stop drinking, seeing a doctor is critical, and not hard to do at all. As long as you have the very sincere desire to *never have another drink*, you should have no problem with this. As a matter of fact, it's time to celebrate! If you have made that commitment, the rest is downhill. Take pride in your decision to stop drinking, and empower yourself to regain control of your life, beginning with your mind and body. See? You are looking better to yourself already!

You can stop drinking with minimal assistance from your doctor, but *you do need your doctor's assistance*. Do not underestimate the affect that alcohol has had on your system. No matter how little you have been drinking, your body has built up some degree of dependence. Ignoring this fact will make the process of quitting much more difficult and risky, and you want to do everything that you can to make it easy.

So, go see a doctor. Doctors are good people and most of them have a deep-rooted and intense desire to help you, and they will; but you need to prepare for the visit.

Surprisingly, few doctors feel comfortable addressing alcohol abuse. It is outside of their symptom/diagnosis/ remedy way of thinking, and it involves very personal things that scare them too. They usually refer patients to a doctor or staff associated with a substance abuse facility, which makes sense since that is their specialty. However, that is not necessarily what you want to do. You want to stop drinking in the privacy of your home, and you recognize the need for medical assistance.

First of all, eliminate your doctor's concern by approaching the subject in a direct and unemotional manner. You have diagnosed your symptoms and have determined that you are abusing alcohol and want to stop. You are confident in the approach that you are taking and are happy to discuss your plans in detail, but what you really need is help with the physical aspects of withdrawal.

When you state that, most doctors will look at you with a secret sigh of relief and with admiration for your strength in making that decision. You will see it in their faces.

Now, your doctor will need to know some things, so be prepared to tell her how much you are drinking each day, and be honest! The medication she prescribes will be based on what you tell her. Don't worry about shocking her. You won't, but accuracy is important because she will want to match your medication with what your body is used to from all the self-medicating that you have been doing.

Self-medicating is a big term among shrinks and counselors who are convinced that drinking alcohol is our way of *medicating our emotional wounds*. It took me about a year to accept that, but now I'm pretty convinced that they are right. Alcohol is a way of hiding unhappiness. It's critical to uncover the source of that sadness so that you can concentrate on repairing your life.

Also, use this time with your doctor to discuss *proper* ways of treating depression. Tell him that you are depressed, or that you are nervous and anxious all the time and need relief from that feeling. You may be sugar-sensitive and that is why you crave alcohol. Another theory is that some alcoholics have attention deficit disorder which was never properly diagnosed when they were children. All of these are possible reasons that you are attracted to the effects of alcohol.

Your doctor can help determine if you have a physical condition that causes your craving for alcohol. Remember the question "Why do I drink?" Try to answer that question, and ask your doctor for help. I mentioned medication. You *want* medication. You are there to get medication, unless it is not medically safe for you to do so. This may be a point of controversy, but I firmly believe that medication is *helpful* if not *essential* for what you are about to do.

Doctors agree too. In a recent review of pharmacological treatments for alcohol intoxication, withdrawal, and dependence, Liskow and

Goodwin (1987) concluded that the drugs of choice for treating withdrawal are the benzodiazepines. Examples are Librium, Valium, Serax, and Ativan. [8]

You will have some degree of alcohol withdrawal syndrome. Mild forms of the syndrome include tremulousness, seizures, and hallucinations, typically occurring within six to forty-eight hours after the last drink. A more severe reaction, delirium tremens (the DTs), involves profound confusion, hallucinations, and severe autonomic nervous system overactivity. These "major shakes" can be highly dangerous in people with severe alcohol dependency. These lovely tremors typically occur forty-eight to ninety-six hours after the last drink.

This is not intended to scare you, but to make you aware that your body may react in some "not so positive" ways. That is why you need to have a doctor involved to help prevent any of these uglies from occurring and to make your detoxification period as comfortable as possible. The DTs in any shape or form are bad. Although not necessarily painful, they are a constant reminder that your nervous system is screaming for alcohol, and they are uncomfortable, to say the least. That's why we need the medication.

Don't be confused. Medication is only for your recuperation time. You don't want to replace one addiction with another. The medication's purpose is to diminish the side effects of alcohol withdrawal so you can begin rebuilding your life. That's really important.

8 National Institute on Alcohol Abuse and Alcoholism, Quarterly Publication No. 5, http://www.niaaa.nih.gov/publications/aa05.htm

Based on your degree of self-medication and your basic physical makeup, you and your doctor should be able to come up with a safe way to ease the discomfort of withdrawal. Also, while you are there, ask for a basic medical examination. It is possible that you have already caused damage to your body, and a simple blood test will reveal if there is something physical going on that you need to repair. Don't chicken out on this. More than likely, you will see that although your blood count is not normal, your body has not incurred permanent damage. This knowledge will encourage you to go further. See? More reasons to celebrate!

It is interesting to note here that the statistics are against outpatient medical detoxification (which is what you are doing). Research shows that it is "an effective, safe, and low-cost treatment for patients with mild-to-moderate symptoms of alcohol withdrawal." However, the data from the same study (Hayashida et al. 1989)[9] indicate that inpatient detoxification was more effective than outpatient detoxification: "At the six-month follow-up, those treated as inpatients reported significantly greater improvement in their drinking behavior, despite having been measured as more impaired than the outpatient group at the time of admission." I believe this is largely due to the ever-present support that this group was provided. Do not underestimate the importance of support from a group or individuals. It is the primary reason for Alcoholics Anonymous' successes. AA is a major network of people who share the same problem, in this case alcohol abuse.

9 Ibid

Find a support group or friends who *understand* your goals regarding drinking though they may not *share* your goals. At least find someone who can empathize with what you are going through. You may have to search for your support group or person, or they may be people very close to you. Whatever your situation, have a confidant that you can talk with. A shrink or counselor does nicely here, if you feel comfortable in that environment.

Pay no attention to the low success ratings of outpatient detoxification. You can stop drinking on your own. It is safe, costs a lot less, and may be much easier. It is just new. I'd much rather recuperate in the comfort of my own home than in a hospital, wouldn't you? Not to mention the embarrassment. Remember though, it goes back to *desire*. As long as you have the sincere desire to *never take another drink*, you will be fine.

One more thing, if you feel uncomfortable discussing this personal matter with your regular physician, go to another one. There are lots of doctors in the world, and this is pretty standard stuff, so find a doctor (in the yellow pages if you have to) and call and schedule an appointment for *anxiety*. Anxiety is a very descriptive term for what you are experiencing. There is anxiety associated with your desire to drink, and there is a lot of anxiety caused by your drinking. So go get treatment for your anxiety! We know the symptoms, diagnosis, and remedy, but need to talk with a doctor.

Careful here. No excuses. Don't start in about medical costs, insurance doesn't pay, or I don't have the money. That's ridiculous. Even if you don't have insurance, you are talking about anywhere from $50 to $150, depending on your doctor and if you do the blood test. This is the best way that you can spend your money right now. I'd guess that there is *nothing in your life more important than this* for you to spend your money on. Not to mention the fact that you spend that much in a week or two on booze!!!

The first thirty days are the most difficult time in the process. Once you go through detox and are feeling really healthy, the advantages of sobriety become obvious. Alcohol becomes less and less attractive to you. Get through the first thirty days, conquer your fears and cravings, and accept the changes in your life so that you will *never have another drink*.

> *It's stressful to drink every day. I know because I've done it. It's hard to plan an eight- to ten-hour workday knowing that you have to go that long without a drink. There again, more stress. It's awful! Planning where and when your next drink will come from causes anxiety in itself.*

Now the important stuff:
How do you prepare?

Think of this as a three-step process. Basically the whole process is a matter of analyzing yourself. It takes a lot of time and consideration, but it's important to understand your way of thinking, why you are thinking it, and ways to change your thought processes and your behavior.

Analyze Your Upbringing

There are many theories/controversies about why we become dependent on alcohol. Try to understand why you have turned to alcohol as a stress remedy. Is it hereditary? If so, how much? Does our environment cause it? If so, is that our present environment or our past?

Chapter 3

Take a Three- or Four-Day Sabbatical!
(Relax and cleanse your body)

It's time to get serious.

This is the beginning of the end. You are really doing it! This next step is something that you prepare for and actually look forward to doing. This will be the time that you set aside to prepare your body for sobriety and will be the beginning of your recuperation (both physically and mentally).

You likely have a great deal of stress in your life or you wouldn't be drinking, right? You need a break! Take it! No matter what you have to do to get the time, do it. Yes, calling in sick is okay here.

You may want to discuss your decision to stop drinking with your employer, depending on your relationship. Many corporations now have employee assistance programs in place that may simplify things for you. However, if you want to keep your recovery a secret, you can do that too. You need only three to four days, so a long weekend will suffice. You figure that out, but set aside a few days for your recovery time, if at all possible.

Basically, plan your R&R time knowing that you won't be feeling great and may even have some times when you feel sick. This will be especially hard for young parents or not-so-young parents with child responsibilities. The demands of children, as parents know, are great, so arrangements need to be made for them. It is difficult, but you have to find a way. Can they stay with friends or family? Whether or not your significant other is supporting you here, you need to be creative and find the time for yourself. At the very least, tell your children that you are sick and will need to stay in bed. Occupy them as you would if you really were sick, because remember, you may be.

Don't be frightened about the being sick part. You are only going to experience symptoms that will occur as a result of *not* drinking. You are not being sick, you are being healthy. Like it or not, your body has adjusted to *some* amount of liquor and many of your organs *need* it to function. Symptoms that may occur are stomachaches, diarrhea, dehydration, fever, chills/sweats, and, of course, those familiar shakes. None of these are particularly painful, but they are certainly uncomfortable. This is not the end of the world and in a few days you will feel like a new person. Also, you are going to have plenty to do and think about, so you will do fine.

Now prepare yourself mentally. You can really have a lot of fun with this. This will be your time to think about anything that you want. You can totally "veg out" on *Talk Soup* (I love that show on E!) or you can go to the library and do some reading on alcoholism, depression, grieving, sibling rivalry, travel, anything that you want. I recommend a good mix where you alternate between some really thoughtless activities like mindless TV, videos, or computer games and then graduate to some thought-provoking stuff like reading *Seven Habits of Successful People* or other motivational books or audiotapes. CNN is a good place to go for a quick look at what's going on in the world so you feel like you know something. That's a good thing.

I like to read books that are politically opinionated because they're fun, but still educational. That may not interest you, but make an attempt to know as much as you can about *something*. It doesn't matter what it is. We all have different interests and likes. Pick something and start learning about it. It's easy, entertaining, and, I believe, therapeutic.

Remember that you must have made the decision that you will never take another drink, and you have to visualize yourself managing a stressful life, doing it all, and doing it sober. When you get a rush, a feeling that this is so right, and that this is the time to take that step for yourself and your family, GO. Start seeing yourself going through the day without drinking, feeling better, handling problems better, and having the respect of your children, co-workers, and spouse. The benefits are overwhelming. Now, let's get your body ready.

First, prepare your food supply.

Go to the grocery store and stock up on Gatorade, water, and maybe a little cranberry juice. Gatorade is probably the best thing for you, so get a variety of flavors and plan to drink one to two of the liter-size bottles per day. Plain water is also good, but stay away from carbonated drinks and fruit juices. The acid in the fruit juices can upset your stomach and the carbonated soft drinks can cause irritation. You can probably have a little cranberry juice (think of it as dinner) or another juice that is low-acid. Also buy some chicken broth, Jell-O, and other bouillon soups. There are a lot of really good instant soups like onion broth, vegetable broth, and beef broth. Check out the soup section and pick out several of your favorites (tons actually). They'll come in handy later.

Now you are ready. Schedule a date, and make it soon. You are now SO READY to begin your new life. Get pumped. In less than a week you will have an entirely new perspective on life, definitely worthy of a celebration.

How are you going to celebrate? Think about it. Come up with some way to reward yourself after your sabbatical/fast. A movie? New outfit? Gourmet meal? Manicure or pedicure? Think of a reward that you will truly enjoy and look forward to having it or doing it.

I'm challenged by finding enjoyable ways to spend my time that do not cost money and that also work toward the accomplishment of other goals in my life. Some of them sound so simple and silly, but if I get enjoyment from them, I'm going to do them.

I like to go to the library, for example. It is amazing how much information is at my fingertips in the library. Everybody is nice and quiet and respectful. It's a good place. I really like the quiet part.

I play games with my kids. I'm not a big video game person but it's amazing how happy it makes my children when I share something like that with them. Throwing the football, swimming, playing a board game, or doing simple activities with your children is extremely enjoyable and productive. There is no replacing time with your children or other loved ones.

Now, GO.

You have your time, groceries, game plan, and your reward, and you are ready to stop drinking. Do it with the knowledge and commitment that you will never have another drink. No matter how long you live. Good Luck!

Chapters Five through Seven

These three chapters are the "meat of the matter" when it comes to my philosophies on not drinking. As I said, I mentally organize them in threes, and within each principle, I set three things to remember so they are readily available in my mind. No lists. Here they are.

Chapter 4

Make Three New Habits

A habit, according to the dictionary, is a behavior pattern acquired by frequent repetition. See that? A behavior pattern acquired by frequent repetition.

That means that if you want to change a current pattern of behavior or habit in your life, you just have to replace that behavior with different actions, frequently repeat those actions (for twenty-one days) and your behavior changes. Does that make sense? There's also a domino effect because you are doing good and positive things for your mind, body, and family, and those things create new opportunities for you to do even more good and positive things for your mind, body, and family. It is so cool.

For example, one new habit that I have formed is looking up words in the dictionary. Such a simple little thing, but it's amazing how thought provoking that can be. As I come across words that I don't understand, or if I need help communicating my thoughts, I go to the dictionary. Besides expanding my vocabulary, it's enlightening to learn the true meaning of words.

Try it. You may find that it's fun, and it's an easy habit to cultivate. Look up one word a day for twenty-one days, form the habit, and see if your vocabulary and communication skills improve.

> *The neat thing about habits is that they are little or big things that we just DO! And as long as they are positive and good for us, our behavior will become positive and good for us, too. It's that simple.*

Now that you have the idea, think of three small changes that you can make in your everyday life. Think of things that will make you feel good about yourself and that you will eventually do without thinking.

Here are some habits that I created for myself that helped in my desire for sobriety.

Drink nonalcoholic beer WHENEVER you want.

Forget the calories on this one. There is no fat in beer and the seventy calories are well worth it to make you feel that you are being a little devilish. I love nonalcoholic beer. It really helps on the social scene and is also a good replacement for those glasses of wine while cooking dinner, having a few beers working on that project, or whatever.

We know that drinking has become a habit for us, and we need to change our habits, right? So take baby steps by beginning with the beverage that most needs to change. Keep your beer, but make it nonalcoholic beer.

One of the scary things about sobriety is the not-drinking effect that it will have on your social life. Nonalcoholic beer is great for this. You are drinking beer so it reduces that irritating question about why you are not drinking. You will still see those raised eyebrows with the question, "Not drinking?" so be prepared. Keep a low profile and when asked you can answer simply, "No, thanks," or "Doctor's orders," or you may want to elaborate with something like. "I'm going to put that stuff down for a while. It's bad for you, you know." That's pretty straightforward and honest.

Simply state that you don't want to drink anymore. Make it a nonevent. You don't want to discuss your reasons/goals at this time. Remember that your not drinking may be intimidating to your friends and work colleagues, so you don't want to get into a debate with them. Answer their question and move the conversation forward.

There is a real plus here, too. Remember that look of admiration that your doctor gave you when you announced that you wanted to stop drinking? You will see a lot of that in these social situations. Sometimes the admiration is masked by jealousy, but it is there just the same. Feel good about yourself and your decisions but don't *gloat*. Gloating is a natural tendency but is very dangerous at this fragile time of your sobriety.

The nonalcoholic beer approach for replacing alcohol is another point of controversy. Doctors, as well as some AA members, say to stay away from anything that looks or tastes like alcohol. The fear is that it is a temptation and is only a step away from drinking the real thing.

I disagree. I can drink nonalcoholic beer all day long and feel like I'm partying, only in a much healthier way. I like having my beer, and I still can. One time a friend of mine confused our beers at a bar one night. She asked which was mine; I wasn't sure so she tasted both to determine which one was hers. She couldn't tell. I thought it was so funny. It was a great moment for me because one of two things had happened: either she clearly had already had too much to drink, or I had indeed proved that there was no difference in the tastes of our beers. Either way, the irony of the situation amused me (wasted on anyone else in the bar, but you get used to that, too).

There is some amount of liquor in nonalcoholic beer (approx. 0.5 percent). That small amount of alcohol has never hurt me, and both my doctors (physician and psychologist) say, "Go for it." Is it a crutch? Probably. Does it work? It did for me.

> *I use the word* DRINKERS *instead of* ALCOHOLICS. *To me the term alcoholic is negative and, frankly, not very well defined. Yes, it is the addiction to alcohol, but when that addiction is conquered, am I still an alcoholic? The clinical definition says yes, but I don't feel like an alcoholic. I don't crave it any longer, and although I was clearly abusive with it at one time, I don't need it to survive. Quite the opposite.*

The point is, don't get hung up on the alcoholism terminology. If you feel strongly that you are an alcoholic, and it helps you to see yourself that way, that's fine. If you don't, that's fine, too. I am someone who once abused alcohol but has made the decision to take it out of my life. Call it what you want.

One caution about socializing with your drinking friends, don't plan to stay out too late. Happy hour is fine, but after a point, people start repeating themselves and acting a little goofy, and that's when it's time to go home and enjoy something else.

Here's where the habits come in handy. Go rent a video, take your children somewhere fun, go home and read, watch TV, or whatever. Remember, *plan* to go home around 9:00 P.M. or 10:00 P.M., have something planned to do (maybe one of your newly formed habits or self-indulgences), and enjoy your time. Think about how everybody in that bar is going to feel in the morning while you are going to wake up to a bright and promising day.

Take your bath/shower at nighttime instead of in the morning.

This one is a good one for me for several reasons. I make a big deal out of my bath. I buy tons of candles, and burn them three to four times a week and spend only about $15–$20 a month, well worth the relaxation and serenity that they provide. My bath relaxes me much better than the usual bottles of wine that I used for relaxation when I was drinking, and I'm productive at the same time. Also, it gives me something to do instead of sitting around wishing that I could drink.

There is nothing wrong with enjoying a nonalcoholic beer or wine while you do this either, by the way (my opinion again).

After my bath, I dry my hair and roll it up on the little pink rollers that I used over twenty years ago. It is great to wake up in the morning with all that done! I can be ready in as little as ten minutes and it makes my mornings much more enjoyable. By the way, mornings had become my favorite time to drink, so this really helped me to get going and start my day without booze. I eventually got so I didn't even think about my morning wine because I was too busy getting things done and starting my day.

Keep a journal.

When I'm facing really difficult decisions, it helps me to sit down with a journal every night and just write. I do it off and on, but when I do "journal" I commit to write for at least seven days and after that I determine if I'll go on for another twenty-three days. I have never kept a journal for more than thirty days, but some people keep them for years. It really helps to clarify situations and helps me make decisions. For one thing, concentrating on a problem enough to write about it an average of ten minutes a day is a lot of thinking.

Also, looking back only a few days can keep things in perspective for me. Sometimes my emotions take over, and seeing how I saw something early in the situation can help me maintain my reason.

A good rule for this is to commit to write *something* every day, even if it is simply the date and the words "too tired to write." If that's all you feel like writing, that's fine. The next night you may feel like filling several pages.

I found that keeping a journal offered the solitude that I needed. I complained that I didn't get enough "alone time" to collect my thoughts and meditate. I was surprised when keeping a journal filled that void. I was able to concentrate on my thoughts much more easily when I sat down and wrote them out.

If you are searching for a way to know yourself, keep a journal for at least a short period of time. It requires some discipline, but the rewards far outweigh any inconveniences.

Multiply your time.

I love to do this, probably due to my time compulsion. I love to think of productive activities that I can do in parallel. I watch the evening news while I'm doing my nails. That's so productive since I'm learning the latest current events and doing a hygiene task at the same time.

Cooking dinner while helping with homework, listening to audiotapes during drive time, and concentrating on an upcoming sales presentation while making copies at school have all worked for me. You will think of your own, and there are thousands. The key is to match a mindless task (manicure, making copies) with one that requires thinking. It works, and you are mentally stimulated as well as proud of your accomplishments.

Eat nonfat yogurt at bedtime.

This is my favorite one because it's not fattening, and it's something that I look forward to every night. I feel really good when my children are in bed after a long day, the dinner dishes are done, and the coffeepot is ready for the next morning. My day is ending and it's my time to relax and watch cable TV and eat my yogurt *in bed* (yes, that's part of it too). This habit makes me feel really proud of my life and, oh yeah, I'm celebrating another good long, productive day.

Make a habit of saving money in small ways.

This is a fun thing to do and can involve the whole family. Goals associated with saving money are enjoyable and, while they may require a little effort, the end result is good. You save money and are proud of your accomplishments while building a little team spirit among family members, if they are involved.

I go to the library instead of buying books, only splurge on fast food if I have a coupon, make cookies instead of buying them, and save change in a jar. There are many habits that you can develop that will save money and reinforce your positive attitude toward small accomplishments.

Put candles everywhere.

The next time that you deserve a reward, do some shopping and pick up some candles. Two or three candles in a room can really change the atmosphere. Candles have a calming effect; they create a soothing atmosphere and smell good too. Put some around the bathtub, next to your bed, or in your kitchen. It doesn't matter where you put them as long as you enjoy them.

Make your own habits! Think about your lifestyle and think of things that you can do semi-automatically that will bring you self-satisfaction and relaxation. There are thousands of little habits that you can create, but the key word is *create.* They have to be *yours.* Think about different ways to relax, different ways to celebrate, and different ways to enjoy your time.

More little habits:

- Get an eye-pillow and spend ten to fifteen minutes a day resting.
- Enjoy your bath. It's not a chore; it's an opportunity for solitude.

- Take your pet for a walk every day.
- Plant a rosebush so you have fresh flowers to cut and bring indoors.
- Read something informative every day.
- Have something to read in your car when you are waiting on kids.
- Pray and/or read the Bible every day.
- Turn the TV off!
- Send a nice note to someone every week, even if it's to the dog.
- Make your own fresh juice and other drinks (fresh grape juice with soda and lemons, yum).
- Dry your sheets (and some clothes) on a clothesline. It saves energy and makes you feel "earthy."

Let me hear your new habits. Everyone can benefit from sharing. Please send us an email at:

www.LikeYourselfAgain.com

Chapter 5

Self-Indulgences/Feel-Good Habits

We all get down. We have good days and bad days. That is how our bodies work. Our bodies are very cyclical, meaning that everything inside us moves around in an orderly and routine manner. When we get upset, the chemical balance in our brain is disturbed and it affects the way we feel. Understanding what is going on in our minds and bodies is very helpful.

While most people cannot really *understand* all the scientific facts related to the human brain, there are some fascinating theories on how we can affect our brain chemistry through diet, exercise, meditation, prayer and in other ways. It all makes sense.

So, what do you do when you get down? Think about it and have on hand (mentally) at least three things that you can do that you know will make you feel better. Basically, plan for your down times.

One of the first things that I do is put a time limit on it! I say, okay, I know that I'm down, so I'm *really* going to be down.

Decide just how long your bad mood should last (depending on the main reason that you are down, of course). Some bad moods only deserve a few hours, but others could last well into the next day. Be specific. Determine how long you are going to be down to the hour. It may be that you are going to feel down until tomorrow at 2:00 P.M. If you have really got a lot of nasty stuff that you have to do, you can extend a bad mood for up to a week.

After you have set your time limit, then you just wallow in your bad mood. Get into it. You can just feel bad and act mad, and you don't even have to be nice to people if you don't want to. After all, things are bad for you right now. You've got a lot of problems, right? Live in that self-pity as long as you need to, but when the time is up, it's all over. If you estimated your time properly (you will get better with practice), you will be really sick of being down, and ready to start smiling and being nice to folks again. Works for me.

Okay, how do you survive between now and the end of your down time? This is when you resort to your feel-good habits. Be prepared for the down times, recognize them when you are having them, and resort to one of your three feel-good habits to make you feel better.

Sometimes I think that I simply cannot get out of bed in the morning because my life is such a wreck, and there is absolutely nothing to look forward to in the upcoming day. Depression. This is when I mentally review my self-indulgences and plan my day accordingly. Be sure to plan for the self-indulgences, because I've learned that sometimes looking forward to them is half the fun (remember the planning thing). However, you need to have at least one that you can do with a minute's notice for those times that you need a quick fix. Here are mine.

Do something in the way of self-development.

This can be a wide variety of things. You can do your fingernails, give yourself a facial, take a walk, read about a current event, read a work-related article, or study a new parental theory. The point is that you are doing something productive for yourself, and that's the key. It's for YOU. You will feel good while doing it and after it is over too. There are many ways to improve yourself, some big and some small. Identify things that you like to do and that will improve your self-esteem and do one of them.

I started giving myself pedicures instead of having them done. It sounds goofy, but my feet feel *almost* as good, and I've saved money too.

Do something nice for someone else.

I love this one! It is by far my favorite self-indulgence! It is incredible how easy it is to find something nice to do for someone else. The self-satisfaction and gratification are incomparable. No matter who you are, it feels good to make someone else feel good.

This also is a broad category but can include all kinds of ways to help others. You can mend a pair of pants, bake something for someone, call someone on the telephone, write someone a letter, send someone a card, or buy someone a present. There is almost always a time when someone has had a baby, gotten married, or graduated from school. I especially like to surprise people in this category. It's fun to go shopping for a small gift and deliver it in person if possible. Even if you have to mail the card or present, you have the feeling that you have made (or will be making) someone else's day brighter. It feels good.

Another great thing about this is that you can exercise some creativity and do something that takes some effort but *saves money*. It's easy to pick up baskets and fill them with sentimental things for someone special. Many times you can find items around your house to help fill a basket, like potpourri, candles, makeup samples, books that you have enjoyed, or cologne.

It's also inexpensive to bake some cookies, pick up some small coffee samplers, or chocolate goodies. As I said, the more effort you spend, the better you feel.

Have on hand a favorite food so you can pig out.

This one's pretty simple. While it sounds a little dangerous because we are trying to remember our doctor's advice about fruits, vegetables, and all that healthy stuff, often it is healthier from a mental/emotional standpoint to go ahead and do something that's just not necessarily good for you.

Hopefully, you will eventually determine a favorite food that doesn't violate the doctor's orders too badly. My current one is baked potato chips with onion dip made from low-fat sour cream (I tried the no-fat sour cream and it just didn't work). Anyway, I can pig out on my chips and dip "pretty good" for about six to eight grams of fat, well worth it from an emotional standpoint. Go ahead. REBEL.

Take a nap.

I love naps, but only in moderation. Naps can be dangerous if you are depressed, so you don't want to make a daily thing of this, but once or twice a week can be fun. I think of naps as the ultimate high.

Think about it. You admitted that you drank to escape, to not have to think about your problems anymore, to make things stop for a little while. That's what naps do. You totally escape. You are relaxed to the point that you can sleep and indulge in its luxury. How totally self-indulgent. Naps! I love them.

Just as with drinking, when you wake up, your problems are all still present, but you are rested, your mind is clear, and you feel better. If you drank before your nap, you would wake up feeling bad, the problems would still be there, and you'd probably just get back into the drinking mode. Waking from naps after a restful sleep feels good. You have had your escape, it's good for your body, and you can enjoy the rest of the day. Try it, but remember, only in moderation. If you sleep too much during the day, you will increase your depression, it will get your nighttime sleep out of whack, and it is not a positive relaxation. Only on occasion.

Do outside things.

What is it about the outdoors that makes us feel good? Fresh air is probably an obvious answer, and appreciating nature and God's work is probably another. Have you ever asked yourself that question, and does it make you feel better to be outside? I think that typically it does. It does for me anyway, and I see it in my children as well.

Do stuff outside. Planting flowers, taking a walk, or just sitting outside can often improve your perspective. I never enjoyed gardening when I drank; that was something for hired people to do. Now the pride that I take in replenishing my flowers and keeping my yard nice is priceless. I see my accomplishment every time I leave or enter my home, and it is such a satisfying feeling.

The main thing to keep in mind with self-indulgences is that you have to have them mentally handy for down times. Everyone has such times. Even if you are a highly successful, perfectly healthy and happy individual with no vices, you will have bad moments and bad days. Remembering your self-indulgences and concentrating on an activity tied to them will help! It's really pretty simple. When you wake up in the morning (or whenever your down moment occurs), just shift your thinking toward a positive activity (the chip-and-dip concept is possible on the positive side), and you will get through it and usually end up in a pretty good mood.

Down times are pretty easy to identify, so just know that that's what you are going through and get busy. By the way, it's okay to go ahead and be down when you are doing whatever you have chosen. That's part of the therapy!

Enjoy your bout of self-pity all the time that you are pigging out, or being brutal on your feet while giving yourself a pedicure, or whatever. Before you know it, you will begin feeling the results of your decision (and hopefully some productivity), and you will start feeling good about yourself again.

A dear friend of mine wrote this poem. It really helps me remember the important things when I'm down.

Training Ground

I don't want to wonder
As my life goes rushing by
About the roads not taken
Or the tears that I have cried

I don't want to live
Always chained unto my past
I want to hear the music
And make the rhythm last

I want to live today
As if I knew I'd die tonight
For then I'd treat everyone with love
No matter who was right

I savor every moment
Of the life that I've been given
For this is but a training ground
Preparing us for Heaven

–Dan Skognes

Chapter 6

Your Three Passions (These are BIG)

Your passions are simply the most important things in your life. You will change them over time, but you won't likely change them often. These are the things that motivate you and make you happy.

> PASSION: "1: *often cap*: the sufferings of Christ between the night of the Last Supper and his death 2: strong feelings: *also pl*: the emotions as distinguished from reason."

This is a great word and I especially like the reference to Christ. It describes the things most important in my life, but the intensity of the word is so well defined by its association with Jesus and His love for us. I also like the part about "*as distinguished from reason.*"

Religion and spiritual beliefs are a passion for most of us. It is very rewarding to share our beliefs with others and to help in small ways to improve life in our community. Involvement in church brings so much self gratification and spiritual uplift. (Everyone knows that already, right?)

What are your passions? Family? Church? Job? What matters to you most? What are your favorite goals? Go back to Chapter One and reread the poem about risks. Answer the questions about risks, especially the one about what you would do if you had only six months left to live.

This question helped me identify my passions. After a great deal of thought, I believe that I would spend as much time as I could watching my son play golf with my daughter by my side. Time with my children and preparing them and myself for my upcoming journey would be my highest priority.

> *It is easy to say that we are passionate about our children, parents, and loved ones. We want our children to grow up and lead productive, happy lives, and our daily behavior has a direct effect on that, whether we like it or not. It is easier to work hard for goals that we are passionate about. In turn, our happiness brings a great deal of warmth and happiness for our loved ones. Love does make the world go round and it is so easy to spread.*

My personal passions are my children, my job, and this book. Sometimes when I feel overwhelmed and misguided, I only have to pause to remember the most important things in my life, and it gives me an excellent perspective. I often ask myself, "How will this help my children, my job, or my book?" If it doesn't affect any of those things, it's not a big issue.

Sure, there are commitments that you have to keep that are not related to your passions; taxes are a good example. Keep your life in perspective and prioritize your time and mental energy for the things that really matter. If you are doing something that affects your passions, do it with gusto! If not, do the best that you can, but with less stress because you know that it isn't a major issue.

How do you know if something in your life is a passion or just something very important? What makes you feel PASSION in your heart, instead of just warm and fuzzy?

I struggled with this for a while. When identifying the top three things in my life, I need to be general, yet specific at the same time if I am to truly focus on that area in my life. I give the process some thought and some time and figure a few things out.

First of all, I begin to notice my decision-making process and look at the times when I am willing to cross the line and do things regardless of the consequences. If I have enough conviction to do what I feel is the right thing, in spite of the risks, it is usually something associated with my children, my job, or my book.

Take some risks. It's healthy, but don't go crazy. Remember the definition: "as distinguished from reason."

During this thought process, also consider the material in Chapter Two, "Why Do I Drink?" Are you afraid of not achieving your goals? Does it seem like too big a job? Fear is a horrible thing, and can be so debilitating, especially if you are drinking too much and feel insecure about your life already. Don't succumb to the fear; you don't have to. Answer those questions and do what you need to fulfill your dreams.

Many of you probably share my passion for God, our creator. When you have God in your heart, you truly understand the meaning of passion. You may ask, "Why is God not one of her three passions?" He is, and very clearly that shows in my desire and determination to complete this book.

My daughter asked me why I was writing this book, and even though many people had asked the same question, for Bevan, my answer was simple: because I feel like God is telling me to do it. That is how I feel, and I also know that it is with God's grace that I am able to do this. I desperately want to find at least one person who can relate to my experience and benefit from what I've learned. It is sometimes lonely in my quest, but it's never long before I feel God's presence and know that I have a partner, the best partner, my Savior.

I have a dear friend in Kansas City who enjoys her relationship with God in literally all aspects of her life. She is a very happy, successful career trainer and mother. She also teaches Bible study in her church. During one of her visits, she was discussing her struggle with understanding a Bible verse, Philippians 4:6:

> Do not be anxious about anything, but in everything, by prayer and petition, with thanksgiving, present your requests to God.

To be anxious in nothing is pretty simple, but prayerful in all things? That seems selfish. If God expects us to pray for every little thing, what about the really big things? We don't want to look ungrateful, like we want too much. She considered this for some time. Then, one day she saw her three-year-old son attempting to operate the VCR. He was frustrated because the videotape wasn't feeding properly in the machine. After a few tries, he stopped, folded his hands, and prayed, "Please God, make this tape work in the VCR." Carrie immediately understood the Bible verse. When God is truly in our heart, he is with us all the time. It is not selfish, but natural that we include Him in all of our thoughts (and prayers).

We can learn so much from our children and from all of those who enter our lives. Looking at life as an adventure, with every new day bringing us knowledge, hope, and compassion is a wonderful way to look at life.

Examine your soul. Who are you, and why are you on this earth? Listen to God and learn from your surroundings to determine what you are intended to accomplish. Look at history, and at your family background. Many people have ended life-long emotional struggles after learning about their ancestors and what drove them. We are a genetic composite of our ancestors, so learn from the past. You may find this exercise to be very helpful in unlocking the key to your soul. Try it.

Seeing my children enjoying their successes, no matter how small, offers so much gratification, I can truly feel the warmth in my body. That's passion. Completing another chapter of my book, with the hope of helping others provides the same warm and calm feeling. It's a natural high, and one that you will not find in alcohol. Experience it yourself. You will see that concentrating on your passions is so fulfilling, you simply will have no time for alcohol. You are really on your way when that happens.

The reasons to stay sober are beginning to outweigh the benefits (bad word) of drinking. Right? It all makes sense when you find happiness and contentment in sobriety.

Remember the list of reasons why you were frightened by sobriety? Go back and review them. Let's see.

When I did this exercise, I honestly couldn't remember why I was scared. I looked at the list I had written, and it made no sense. Afraid of getting the shakes, not sleeping, the effects on my social life? None of that makes sense to me now. It looks absolutely dumb.

Chapter 7

It's All in Your Mind

Do you know that you can affect your external environment with your thoughts? I am a BIG believer in the power of positive thinking. If you are not, I'd recommend that you do some reading on the topic with an open mind, and consider its validity.

You have a conscious and a subconscious mind. If you constantly feed your *subconscious* mind positive thoughts through your *conscious* mind, your perspective will be positive. You can affect your external environment. Don't get carried away. You can't move objects or make things disappear, but your confidence, conviction, and positive outlook will take you a very long way.

How does it work? It's simple. Your subconscious mind is a big database of thoughts, which your conscious mind feeds it. Your subconscious mind has every experience in your life stored, whether you can remember it or not. It's only natural that when you face decisions, your only reference is past life experience, stored in your subconscious mind. That is who you are. *My father still reminds me, "You are a product of the decisions that you make."*

Try to fill your database with only positive thoughts. You are an honorable and responsible person. You try your best. You are honest. You are loyal. You work hard. You know your job well, and you are good at it. You know that the recommendation that you are making to your boss is a fine one. You know that your new program will benefit your department and your entire company.

Do you see how it works? Because you know something, and believe it strongly, others will believe it too. If they don't, find out why. They may have information that you don't have, so listen with an open mind. A situation you would have considered negative in the past now becomes an opportunity to learn something new. At the very least, you can show some creativity, an open mind, and the willingness to change. See? Even if your idea is rejected, there is a positive side.

Always search for the positive. There *is* a positive side to everything, a silver lining to every cloud. Find it, and *that* is the data that you store.

> *Believe that things can happen and they will. Feed your mind positive thoughts, visualize positive outcomes, and you will be amazed at the effect. Positive thinking is a powerful thing.*

While this may sound crazy, it works for a lot of people. Try it. Imagine positive experiences that are going to happen to you. Visualize attaining your goals and enjoying the rewards of your hard work. This is the way you should think about the material in this book. You can change the direction of your life by believing that it can happen and by seeing yourself as a healthy, successful, and confident person. That is what you will become when you make the commitment to never have another drink and believe that it will happen. When negative events happen, try to find the positive in them. It's hard sometimes, but you must try. Before you know it, you will have developed the habit of seeing things positively, and that is what your world will become.

The Importance of Planning

Planning is a good habit to develop. It is important so that you can visualize your successes and is important for the little things too.

As a sales manager, I used to ask a class of new hires the question, "Why do we plan?" It's a good icebreaker and encourages quick participation among the group. It was amazing the number of answers I got before I heard what I was looking for.

Someone always volunteered, "to be more organized," "to make sure that we get everything done." After a pause, someone would suggest that we plan in order to be more strategic with our processes, as a vehicle of communication for team support, feedback, and presentations. "Planning helps quantify a process," "to understand goals," others would add. The group continued on and on but still no one gave the answer I was waiting to hear. The group eventually became impatient, and, almost always, everyone had contributed to the discussion and they would ask, "What else?"

It amazes me even today, but the answer is to increase our confidence. WOW, isn't it true? Planning does all of the above, *plus* it increases our confidence. What a neat thing.

When we are organized, strategic, and have good communication, we are more confident. So, in some form or fashion, make planning one of your daily habits. It can be something as simple as just *thinking* of three things which you are going to accomplish in the day, or you can go crazy with it, like me, and have color-coded lists with estimated completion times, and a full twelve hours planned. My shrink says that I'm pretty compulsive in the time area, so I've tried to *reduce* my time management tendencies.

Time.

Time is such a neat thing and something I have come to really appreciate with sobriety. When I was drinking, I was so compulsive with my time, it seemed I couldn't get enough into each day, but I really didn't enjoy time. Dr. Eubanks taught me to "stop and smell the flowers." (Actually the expression is "stop and smell the roses," but I'm not a roses fan, so I made it flowers instead.) It took a lot of practice, but now I can truly enjoy the passing of time.

Think about it. When you are drinking, the drug stimulates your mind and body. Even if you are not drinking and are only hungover, your nervous system is shattered enough to keep you nervous. There are those nasty shakes that you are worried about people noticing, so you have a drink before the Little League game. Then you sit there and wonder if anyone can smell the alcohol or if they can tell that you have been drinking. Rather than enjoying watching your child participate in an activity, you are a bundle of nerves.

All of that goes away after you stop drinking. It took me about a year to understand what Dr. Eubanks meant, but he's so right. Sitting in the stands, looking on as a proud mother, self-assured with my own decisions and lifestyle, I enjoy the passing of time and appreciate the rare moments when I can sit back and value all that I have in life.

Time is such a valuable commodity. Learn to enjoy the passing of time. I could only do that after I stopped drinking. That feeling of "Oh, I feel good about myself" just doesn't come when you are drinking. It didn't for me, anyway. Eat an apple, drink some Ovaltine, do something healthy before you set out on one of these tasks. It's a good reminder of your commitment to a healthy mind and body, and you will begin to look forward to enjoying the moments.

These are little strategies that get you through the day. Remember the old saying, "Change is the spice of life"? It is good for us to make changes, especially if we're depressed, or are trying to improve our behavior. Ideally, the good habits that we develop will help us through our days, keep us occupied, and make us feel more productive. At first, though, concentrate on changing three details of your day, anything, no matter how small or large. Take a different route home from work, go to a different grocery store, or find new specialty shops to visit, but change your routine somehow.

Mental Energy/Emotional Energy

Just as you concentrate on the energy level in your body, you can just as easily maintain control over your mental or emotional energy.

Some days you wake up feeling very enthusiastic and energetic, and other times you wonder how you can get through the day. When you identify your mood and plan your day accordingly, you are deciding how to spend your emotional energy. In other words, if you feel down (depressed) you try to *indulge* in something that will make you feel better and increase your energy level. When you wake up feeling good and happy, you have less to do, but you still need to be conscious of your energy level so that you can maintain a normal flow.

Remember that your conscious brain tells your subconscious brain what to think, so if you feel sluggish, you know that you can increase your mental energy by concentrating on positive activities and in turn feel better about yourself.

Doesn't that make sense? You are regulating or controlling your emotional energy.

Think of emotional energy as a commodity, like time. You want to have an even flow of energy in your mind, just as you do in your body. Spend it wisely. Get excited, sad, mad, happy, as the activities in your day and life provide.

Sometimes you have no control over occurrences in your life that cause anger and grief, and you positively will have those emotions. You know that you can't control that, but you can control the amount of emotional energy that you devote to them. Some things are easier than others are, and just as there are uncontrollable tragedies, there are also positive events. Look for them. Balance your emotional energy as much as you can.

Strong feelings such as anger, grief, and intense joy require a great deal of emotional energy. That often brings on depression and low energy. That's when it is necessary to create positive feelings to generate energy and counteract the negatives. It's like a bank account. If you make a large withdrawal, you need to replace the energy by depositing positive thoughts.

Plan how you will expend your emotional energy. It may sound crazy but when Scarlett O'Hara said, "If I think about that right now, I'll go crazy. I'll just have to think about that tomorrow," that's actually very healthy. When you are overloaded with stress it's okay to decide to think about it tomorrow. First, ask yourself the question "Does this require action today?" Even though what you're facing is important, it may not be urgent, so don't make it so.

You can even plan *when* to focus on an emotional energy drain. For example, when I know that I'll be busy getting the kids to school and then preparing for and having a conference call at 9:00 A.M., I mentally plan to devote my time to thinking about a known crisis at 11 A.M. sound crazy? It works. Sometimes, circumstances may have changed so that the crisis has decreased in importance. Others may have contacted me, offering assistance or support. Other occurrences may have eliminated the crisis altogether, thereby defusing the situation. At the very least, I have stored the energy to deal with the crisis and have planned my day around it.

Today

I would love to begin this chapter by saying how wonderful my life has become. While I would love to finish this with a final chapter of endless successes and unfailing promises for a long and prosperous life, I cannot. My "Knight in Shining Armor" has not ridden into my life and made every day full of love and family and all the things that matter to me. My children do not have a responsible and loving male role model in their lives.

I wish that I could travel with my children and teach them all that I can in the short time that I have left with them under my roof. I cherish every day, but time passes so quickly and I have so much to do before I send them out into this sometimes cruel and sometimes glorious life. Their happiness means everything to me and I want to affect it in any way that I can. I know that I make mistakes, but I also know that I've made some good decisions too.

I struggle with depression every day. When I find myself with too much time on my hands, I sleep too much. I could go for days without leaving my house if I didn't make a conscious effort to keep busy and to be around people. Sometimes small talk with the folks at my local grocery story is the extent of my social activity for a day. I have a tendency to become reclusive. I don't know where I belong in social settings any longer. I don't "wear" divorce well, so it's easier to stay at home rather than face the scrutiny of other single men, jealous wives, and all those well-meaning friends offering sympathy.

Where do I belong in this world? What will become of me after the kids leave home? I have lots of fears, ideas and definitely some dreams, but I do not know what God has in store for me. I can only trust in Him and have faith that he will show me His way.

Each morning, I spend ten to fifteen minutes evaluating the day ahead of me and praying about it. I play a little game with my subconscious mind. I try to program my mind to have God be the first thing that I think about when I wake up. Do you ever think about that? What is the very first thing that pops into your mind when you wake up? Not the alarm clock, but right after you push that snooze button and roll back over to steal a few more winks. What do you think about then?

I really like it when God is automatically the first thing that I think about. He isn't always, but when He is, I feel his presence so strongly that I know that it's going to be a great day.

In spite of the circumstances of my life, I know that I have SO much. I have healthy and happy children, and I am healthy and happy at least some of the time. I have a wonderful job that I enjoy, a home that I'm proud of, a couple of dogs, a neat church, good friends, and healthy parents. I could go on and on.

But most important, I have my sobriety. I treasure my sobriety because it gives me the confidence and health I need to raise my children and to serve God. As I live each day, I take pride in my sobriety, and I know that *no one* can take that from me. I'm in total control of my life and I have confidence that I'm making each decision with the careful consideration that it requires.

That's what makes my life good. I know in my heart and in my soul that I'm doing the best that I can. That's a big accomplishment! That security gives me more satisfaction than all the wine I ever drank. I have a good life. I have problems but they are far fewer than when I was drinking.

I find comfort and happiness in many things, especially the little moments in life. As my dear friend, Marcy, says, "Do the dog thing." Take them for a walk, throw them a ball, or just watch them. Pets truly live to bring their masters protection and companionship. It amazes me to watch them find such joy in my attention. It warms my heart. Small, unexpected moments of pleasure like these are what matter most to me. There are so many opportunities to look around and enjoy life.

I have my little sitting areas in my home where I go to be alone with my thoughts. I may sit outside in my rocker, or read in my "sitting room," or work on my laptop in my bed (what decadence!); it all depends on my mood. The key word here is MY mood. I take time to be alone with my thoughts—soul searching, as we used to say. I go to these small spaces of sanctuary when I'm angry, sad, happy, and pensive, or just want to relax. It is a small escape that gives me pleasure. I might light candles, sketch on a sketchpad, write in my journal or just sit. Whatever I do, it's an event!

I have also come to appreciate the time that I spend writing in my journal. What began as a dreaded chore now offers me so much insight. By the time I sit down and write about an issue, no matter what it is, the details are clearer, and even if I don't yet know the right thing to do, I feel better armed to make that important decision. This form of communicating gives me a great deal of comfort. Often my entries are in the form of prayer. It's a powerful thing to write a letter/journal entry to God. One of my favorite sayings is, "You are closest to your creator when you are creating." It's so true. Even if I'm creating a document that will never be shared with anyone on earth, I am creating, and I sense a powerful connection with God. That same connection is what has motivated me to write this book. I know that God has a purpose for us all and that my experiences with alcohol are for a purpose. The purpose is still unknown, but I have to believe that sharing my story in hopes of helping others is God's will for me.

My life today is no bed of roses, but it is a good life. I have so much, and the best part is that I've come to appreciate it. I can identify the things that make me happy and the things that bring me down. I avoid the things that bring me down or at least prepare for them and have my reward system in place to get through them. It works for me.

Hopefully it will work for you too. It all begins with sobriety. Please find yours. Don't be intimidated about not drinking; remember, it's not that hard! Once you make up your mind that you want to take alcohol out of your life, the rest is easy. Learn from my mistakes and do not waste another day of your life.

Also remember, I'm praying for you.

Talk With God

When you're all alone and silence is
The only sound you hear
Listen for that still small voice
And know that God is near

He wants to know what's on your heart
He wants to hear your praise
Take the time to talk to Him
For numbered are your days

God cares about the way you feel
He feels your joy and pain
So if you love Him, let it show
And from your sins abstain

Don't take for granted that you have
Another day to live
So live this day like it's your last
Remember to forgive

Talk with God throughout the day
And share your heart's desire
God is waiting there to give
You peace this very hour

-Dan Skognes

Epilogue

October, 2001

I began writing this book in 1997 and completed it in 1999. It was wonderful therapy for me and gave me an invaluable feeling of worth as I suffered through a very difficult time in my life. It is now 2001 and the last section of the book is no longer applicable. I am happy to say that I have met the love of my life and my children do have a wonderful male role model in which to pattern their lives. (It will take them about forty years to see that, but, oh well, that's another book.)

God has so richly blessed my life and I see now that my suffering was all for a better cause. Now my desire is to be obedient to God, to be his servant, and to reach out to help others. On September 11, 2001, our country was viciously attacked, and everyone in America was affected in some way. Whether our lives were affected dramatically or only slightly, I see Americans coming together for a common cause. I see people striving for understanding, for peace, and for the

Something Else. That Something Else is GOD. My pastor says, "You have to be ready to die before you're ready to live," and I believe that with all my heart. My personal relationship with God and his Son, Jesus Christ, has had a tremendous impact on my life, my happiness, my family, and my successes. I will encourage you to find that same serenity. We may not always understand God's actions, but we can always count on his promises, specifically that "He will not forsake us."

My favorite Bible verse (which helped me *many* times during recent years) is found in Romans 5:3–5.

> Rejoice in our sufferings, because we know that suffering produces perseverance; perseverance, character; and character, hope. And hope does not disappoint us.

Isn't that awesome? It is so true. When we experience times of suffering, are we not better, stronger, and wiser because of it? Knowing that we have God's promises, we know that we have hope, and we are only better for our experiences. I love the word of God, the Bible. What an awesome book!

Reviewing my manuscript after over a year, it's fun to see how my passions, self-indulgences, and small habits have changed. My passions today are God, my family, and serving others. I realize now that without God I wouldn't have my family, my job, or anything. That's why it's easy to place Him at the top of my passions list, and then everything else comes together.

I have many new little habits (like reading the Bible daily and changing everyday routines), but my self-indulgences are still exactly the same. Doing nice things for others is still the best therapy for when I'm down; the self-development tactics still work; and it cracks me up that the chip-and-dip strategy still does the trick every time too. Isn't that funny? No matter how much we change, we still stay the same.

So that's my final word. Know your passions, change your habits, and make lifestyle changes. Follow your heart and listen to that still voice inside of you. We are on this earth only for a short time; make something of your life. And again, I am praying for you, EVERY DAY.

About the Author

Becky Nelson continues her long-term career with a global electronics manufacturer of wireless devices. She lives in the Dallas suburb of Coppell, Texas with her husband, Dan, and two children. She is an active member of Fellowship Church in Grapevine, Texas.

Book comments or questions can be sent to
Becky@likeyourselfagain.com